Zoo Pocket Guide

For since the creation of the world God's invisible qualities—His eternal power and divine nature—have been clearly seen, being understood from what has been made, so that people are without excuse.

Romans 1:20

Wasil Science: Zoo Pocket Guide
By Joseph Wasil
Wasil Science, LLC.

From the Wasil Science Creation Creature Feature Series, Volume 60

© Copyright Wasil Science, LLC.2024

Animal Identification and Conservation Guide. Publisher, Wildlife Fact File International Masters Publishers, 1991.

Revelation 4:11

**"Worthy are You, our Lord and God,
to receive glory and honor and power,
for You created all things,
and by Your will they existed and were created."**

Check out these incredible creatures designed by our Lord, and some of the most common zoo animals!

- Lions
- Hippos
- Red Pandas
- Gorillas
- Cheetahs
- Elephants
- Giraffes
- Constrictors

- Red Kangaroos
- Tigers
- Meerkats
- Crocodiles
- Polar Bears
- Peafowl
- Emperor Penguins
- Zebras

LIONS

Creation Creature Features:

- These creatures are large members of the cat family.
- Most wild lions call Africa home.
- These creatures are designed with rosette type spots when they are young.
- Lions eventually grow out of this camouflage as they get older.

Scientific Name: Panthera leo
Habitat: Grasslands
Mass: 420 lbs
Speed: 46 mph
Life Span: 15 years
Conservation Status: Vulnerable
Day Created: Day 6

HIPPOS

Creation Creature Features:

- Hippos are amazing semi-aquatic mammals designed by God to live in Africa.
- These creatures are the third largest land
- mammals behind the elephant and rhinoceros.
- Their name is derived from the Greek term for "river horse".

Scientific Name: Hippopotamus amphibius
Habitat: Sub-Sahara lakes & rivers
Mass: 4,000 lbs
Speed: 19 mph
Life Span: 50 years
Conservation Status: Vulnerable
Day Created: Day 6

RED PANDAS

Creation Creature Features:

- 98% of a red panda's diet is bamboo leaves.
- They eat up to 30% of their body weight every day.
- Designed to be active during the twilight hours until the early hours.
- Similar to the giant panda they have a pseudo-thumb to help grasp branches.

GORILLAS

Creation Creature Features:

- Gorillas are powerful primates living in the forests of Africa.
- These creatures move on all four limbs with most weight supported by their feet and knuckles.
- They are designed with hands that allow them to grasp trees and climb.

Scientific Name: Gorilla beringei

Habitat: Rainforest

Mass: 600 lbs

Speed: 25 mph

Life Span: 40 years

Conservation Status: Endangered

Day Created: Day 6

CHEETAHS

Creation Creature Features:

- These creatures live in Africa and are made for speed.
- For up to a sixth of a mile cheetahs can clock in at about 70 miles per hour.
- God designed cheetahs with tear markings under their eyes to help reduce sunlight glare while hunting.

ELEPHANTS

Creation Creature Features:

- Males stand up to 13 feet tall and weigh up to 15,000 pounds.
- African elephants have much larger ears and are similarly shaped to the African continent.
- Asian elephants are much smaller with ears shaped like the Indian subcontinent.

Scientific Name: Elephantidae
Habitat: Grasslands
Mass: 8,000 lbs
Speed: 25 mph
Life Span: 60 years
Conservation Status: Endangered
Day Created: Day 6

Creation Creature Features:

- Giraffes are the tallest mammals on Earth designed by God Almighty.
- Giraffes call the dry savannahs of Africa home as they roam the open plains and woodlands.
- Excellent eyesight allows them to spot hungry predators from far away.

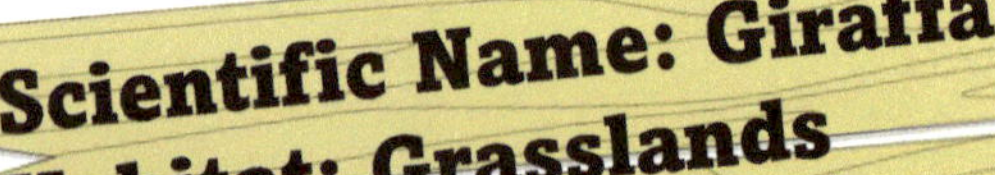
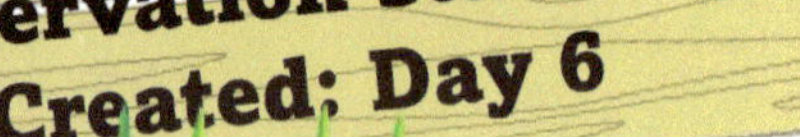

Scientific Name: Giraffa
Habitat: Grasslands
Mass: 2,600 lbs
Speed: 37 mph
Life Span: 25 years
Conservation Status: Vulnerable
Day Created: Day 6

CONSTRICTORS

Creation Creature Features:

- Constrictors are grouped as non-venomous snakes that use strong muscles to stop blood flow in prey.
- Green anacondas are some of the largest snakes in the world.
- Their jaws are not fused together allowing them to expand with elastic tissue.

RED KANGAROOS

Creation Creature Features:

- They have powerful hind limbs helping kangaroos hop huge lengths with amazing efficiency.
- Baby kangaroos are called joeys and weigh less than two grams at birth.
- Their tails are helpful for balance, used for support when moving slowly.

TIGERS

Creation Creature Features:

- Tigers are some of the largest cats in the world designed by our Lord.
- They can embark on long journeys looking for food.
- Tigers are designed with acute senses.
- Tigers rotate their ears like a radar dish to pick up sounds of prey in the forest.

Scientific Name: Panthera tigris
Habitat: Temperate forest
Mass: 650 lbs
Speed: 40 mph
Life Span: 15 years
Conservation Status: Endangered
Day Created: Day 6

MEERKATS

Scientific Name: Suricata suricatta

Habitat: Dry plains

Mass: 1.6 lbs

Speed: 20 mph

Life Span: 14 years

Conservation Status: Least Concern

Day Created: Day 6

Creation Creature Features:

- Meerkats are designed to be reliant on teamwork to survive in the Kalahari Desert.
- Meerkats are a species of mongoose.
- Meerkats dig a large network of burrows.
- God designed the meerkat with the ability to dig burrows up to 10 feet deep often looking for food.

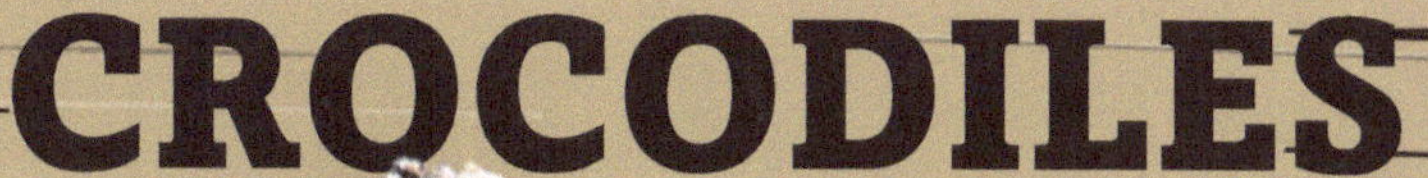

CROCODILES

Creation Creature Features:

- **Crocodiles live along rivers and lakes migrating long distances during the wet season.**
- **Crocodiles are ectothermic and need to avoid extreme temperatures.**
- **The crocodile cannot chew food so it must 'death roll' to twist pieces of the animal off to eat by swallowing.**

Scientific Name: Crocodylidae
Habitat: Saltwater areas
Mass: 2,000 lbs
Speed: 20 mph
Life Span: 60 years
Conservation Status: Vulnerable
Day Created: Day 5

Creation Creature Features:

- Polar bears are the largest land carnivores.
- They are the only bears classified as marine mammals.
- Polar bears have big appetites and can eat 20% of their body weight.
- Cubs are born in carved out snow dens.

Scientific Name: Ursus maritimus
Habitat: Arctic regions
Mass: 990 lbs
Speed: 25 mph
Life Span: 30 years
Conservation Status: Vulnerable
Day Created: Day 6

PEAFOWL

Creation Creature Features:

- God created peafowl as some of the largest of all birds that fly.
- The beautiful feathers covering the tails of a male peacock can be up to five feet long.
- Peafowl inhabit open lowland forests and will flock together during the day and roost up in trees at night.

Scientific Name: Pavo cristatus
Habitat: Open forests
Mass: 10 lbs
Speed: 10 mph
Life Span: 15 years
Conservation Status: Least Concern
Day Created: Day 5

EMPEROR PENGUINS

Creation Creature Features:

- These creatures are aquatic flightless members of the bird classification.
- Emperor penguins are known for their 'COUNTERSHADING' coloration with a white belly and dark back.
- God designed emperor penguins as very hardy withstanding extreme temperatures!

ZEBRAS

Creation Creature Features:

- God created zebras to have unique stripe patterns similar to our fingerprints.
- There are three different species of zebras: the plains zebra, Grevy's zebra, and mountain zebra.
- Zebras are designed with the ability to sleep while standing up.

Scientific Name: Equus quagga

Habitat: Grasslands & Savannahs

Mass: 800 lbs

Speed: 40 mph

Life Span: 20 years

Conservation Status: Near Threatened

Day Created: Day 6

Field Journal

Record your observations and drawings
of your favorite animals at the zoo!

Field Journal

Record your observations and drawings
of your favorite animals at the zoo!

PHYSICS
Wasil Science
Exciting Creation Adventures
from a Biblical Worldview!
Hosted by
Science Teacher
Joseph Wasil
M. Ed.
CHemIStrY
C Carbon 12.011
He Helium 4.00260
I Iodine 126.90447
S Sulfur 32.065
Y Yttrium 88.90585
Biology
All rights reserved.
Fun curriculum supplements & resources for students ages 5+
pairing well with any textbooks!
Wasil Science, LLC.
New Year,
NEW DISCOVERIES!
SCAN ME
Wasil Science
Creation Creature
Feature Series
Cheeta
Joseph Wasil
M. Ed.
Designe
Dinosaurs!
JUST
$10
Wasil Science Jr.
presents
"Gator Explores..."
INSECTS
Joseph Wasil
M. Ed.
Wasil Science, LLC.